CW01266263

THE
JAMES JOYCE
QUOTATION BOOK

Compiled by Andrew Russell

SOMERVILLE PRESS

Somerville Press Ltd,
Dromore, Bantry, Co. Cork, Ireland

©Andrew Russell 2024

Designed by Jane Stark
Typeset in Minion Pro
seamistgraphics@gmail.com

ISBN: 978 1 8382544 90

Printed and bound in the EU

FRONT COVER PHOTO:
James Joyce by Alex Ehrenzweig 1915
(PUBLIC DOMAIN)

THE SUPREME VICE IS SHALLOWNESS.

A Portrait of the Artist as a Young Man

You made me confess
the fears that I have.
But I will tell you also
that I do not fear.
I do not fear to be alone
or to be spurned for another
or to leave whatever I have to leave.
And I am not afraid to make a mistake,
a lifelong mistake and perhaps as
long as eternity too.

A Portrait of the Artist as a Young Man

The present moves from the past, not in to it.

Ulysses

Dear dirty Dublin

'A Little Cloud'
Dubliners

Riverrun, past Eve and Adam's from swerve of shore to bend of bay, brings us by a commodious vicus of recirculation back to Howth Castle and Environs.

Finnegans Wake

> OF ALL THE ENGLISH WRITERS CHAUCER IS THE CLEAREST. HE IS AS PRECISE AND SLICK AS A FRENCHMAN.
>
> Frank Budgen
> *James Joyce and the Making of Ulysses*
> (1934)

> WRITING IN ENGLISH IS THE MOST INGENIOUS TORTURE DEVISED FOR SINS COMMITTED IN PREVIOUS LIVES.
>
> From a letter to Fanny Guillermet

Mr Leopold Bloom ate with relish the inner organs of beasts and fowls. He liked thick giblet soup, nutty gizzards, a stuffed roast heart, liver slices fried with crust crumbs, fried hen cock's roes. Most of all he liked grilled mutton kidneys which gave his palate a fine tang of faintly scented urine.

Ulysses

The heaventree of stars hung with humid nightblue fruit.

Ulysses

'It is a curious thing you know,' Cranly said dispassionately, 'how your mind is supersaturated with the religion in which you say you do not believe.'

A Portrait of the Artist as a Young Man

When the soul of a man is born in this country there are nets flung at it to hold it back from flight. You talk to me of nationality, language, religion. I will try to fly by those nets.

A Portrait of the Artist as a Young Man

> THE OBJECT
> OF THE ARTIST
> IS THE CREATION
> OF THE BEAUTIFUL.
> WHAT THE BEAUTIFUL IS
> IS ANOTHER QUESTION.
>
> *A Portrait of the Artist as a Young Man*

To LEARN

ONE MUST BE HUMBLE.

BUT LIFE IS

THE GREAT TEACHER.

Ulysses

Full many a flower is born to blush unseen.

Ulysses

Snow was falling in every part of the dark central plain, on to the treeless hills softly upon the Bog of Allen, and further westward, softly falling into the dark mutinous Shannon waves.

'The Dead'
Dubliners

They lived and laughed and loved and left.

Finnegans Wake

> YOUR BATTLES INSPIRED ME –
> NOT THE OBVIOUS
> MATERIAL BATTLES
> BUT THOSE THAT WERE
> FOUGHT AND WON
> BEHIND YOUR FOREHEAD.
>
> *From a letter to Ibsen*

It is not my fault that the odour of ashpits and old weeds and offal hangs round my stories. I seriously believe that you will retard the course of civilization in Ireland by preventing the Irish people from having one good look at themselves in my nicely polished looking glass.

Letter 23 June 1906

No-one wanted him: he was an outcast from life's feast.

'A Painful Case'
Dubliners

SHAKESPEARE IS THE HAPPY HUNTING GROUND FOR ALL MINDS THAT HAVE LOST THEIR BALANCE.

Ulysses

The language in which we are speaking is his before it is mine.

A Portrait of the Artist as a Young Man

I WILL TELL YOU WHAT I WILL DO AND WHAT I WILL NOT DO. I WILL NOT SERVE THAT IN WHICH I NO LONGER BELIEVE, WHETHER IT CALLS ITSELF MY HOME, MY FATHERLAND OR MY CHURCH: AND I WILL TRY TO EXPRESS MYSELF IN SOME MODE OF LIFE OR ART AS FREELY AS I CAN AND AS WHOLLY AS I CAN, USING FOR MY DEFENSE THE ONLY ARMS I ALLOW MYSELF TO USE – SILENCE, EXILE AND CUNNING.

A Portrait of the Artist as a Young Man

A MAN OF GENIUS
MAKES NO MISTAKES.
HIS ERRORS
ARE VOLITIONAL
AND PORTALS
OF DISCOVERY.

Ulysses

THINK
YOU ARE ESCAPING
AND YOU RUN INTO
YOURSELF.
LONGEST WAY ROUND
IS THE
SHORTEST WAY HOME.

Ulysses

I WANTED REAL ADVENTURE
TO HAPPEN TO MYSELF.
BUT REAL ADVENTURES,
I REFLECTED,
DO NOT HAPPEN TO PEOPLE
WHO REMAIN AT HOME:
THEY MUST BE SOUGHT
ABROAD.

'An Encounter'
Dubliners

> # The ideal reader suffering from an ideal insomnia.
>
> *Finnegans Wake*

In Ulysses I have recorded, simultaneously, what a man says, sees, thinks, and what such seeing, thinking, saying, does, to what you Freudians call the subconscious – but as for psychoanalysis, it's nothing more or less than blackmail.

Interview *Vanity Fair* March 1922

> I RESENT VIOLENCE OR INTOLERANCE IN ANY SHAPE OR FORM... IT IS A PATENT ABSURDITY ON THE FACE OF IT TO HATE PEOPLE BECAUSE THEY LIVE AROUND THE CORNER OR SPEAK ANOTHER VERNACULAR, SO TO SPEAK.
>
> *Ulysses*

THE DEMAND
I MAKE
FROM MY READER
IS THAT
HE SHOULD DEVOTE
HIS WHOLE LIFE
TO READING MY WORKS.

O DREAD AND DIRE WORD. ETERNITY! WHAT MIND OF MAN CAN UNDERSTAND IT?

A Portrait of the Artist as a Young Man

> EACH LOST SOUL
> WILL BE A HELL
> INTO ITSELF,
> THE BOUNDLESS FIRE
> RAGING IN
> ITS VERY VITALS.
>
> *A Portrait of the Artist as a Young Man*

IRELAND IS THE OLD SOW THAT EATS HER FARROW.

A Portrait of the Artist as a Young Man

'THIS RACE
AND THIS COUNTRY
AND THIS LIFE
PRODUCED ME',
HE SAID.
'I SHALL EXPRESS
MYSELF AS I AM.'

A Portrait of the Artist as a Young Man

Stately, plump Buck Mulligan came from the stairhead, bearing a bowl of lather on which a mirror and razor lay crossed.

Ulysses

> Time's ruins build eternity's mansions.
>
> *Ulysses*

'We were always loyal to lost causes', the professor said. 'Success for us is in the dark of the intellect and of the imagination.'

Ulysses

She respected her husband
in the same way
that she respected
the General Post Office,
something that was
large secure and fixed.

'A Mother'
Dubliners

Silently, in a dream she had come to him after her death, her wasted body within its loose brown graveclothes giving off an odour of wax and rosewood.

Ulysses

THE TASK I SET MYSELF TECHNICALLY IN WRITING A BOOK FROM EIGHTEEN DIFFERENT POINTS OF VIEW AND IN AS MANY STYLES, ALL APPARENTLY UNKNOWN OR UNDISCOVERED BY MY FELLOW TRADESMEN, THAT AND THE NATURE OF THE LEGEND CHOSEN WOULD BE ENOUGH TO UPSET ANYONE'S MENTAL BALANCE.

> A WRITER SHOULD NEVER WRITE ABOUT THE EXTRAORDINARY. THAT IS FOR THE JOURNALIST.
>
> Letter to Djuna Barnes

> 'TIS AS HUMAN
> A LITTLE STORY
> AS PAPER COULD
> WELL CARRY.
>
> *Finnegans Wake*

I AM TOMORROW,
OR SOME FUTURE DAY,
WHAT I ESTABLISHED
TODAY.
I AM TOMORROW
WHAT I ESTABLISHED
YESTERDAY
OR SOME PREVIOUS DAY.

A Portrait of the Artist as a Young Man

THE MOVEMENTS
WHICH WORK REVOLUTIONS
IN THE WORLD
WERE BORN OUT OF
THE DREAMS AND VISIONS
IN A PEASANT'S HEART
ON THE HILLSIDE.

A Portrait of the Artist as a Young Man

> THE SEA,
> THE SNOTGREEN SEA,
> THE SCROTUMTIGHTENING SEA.
>
> *Ulysses*

All moanday,

tearsday,

wailsday,

thumpsday,

frightday,

shatterday

till the fear of the law.

Finnegans Wake

> His heart danced upon her movements like cork upon a bottle.

A Portrait of the Artist as a Young Man

AND THEN I ASKED HIM
WITH MY EYES TO ASK AGAIN
YES
AND THEN HE ASKED ME WOULD I
YES
AND HIS HEART WAS
GOING LIKE MAD AND
YES I SAID
YES I WILL YES.

Ulysses

EVERY LIFE IS IN MANY DAYS,
DAY AFTER DAY.
WE WALK THROUGH OURSELVES,
MEETING ROBBERS, GHOSTS,
GIANTS, OLD MEN, YOUNG MEN,
WIVES, WIDOWS,
BROTHERS-IN-LOVE,
BUT ALWAYS MEETING
OURSELVES.

Ulysses

Love

loves

to

love

love.

Ulysses

> But my body was like a harp and her words and gestures were like figures running upon the wires.
>
> 'Araby'
> *Dubliners*

When a young man came up to him in Zurich and said, 'May I kiss the hand that wrote *Ulysses*?' Joyce replied, somewhat like King Lear, 'No, it did lots of other things too.'

Richard Ellman *James Joyce* (1982)

> THERE IS NO HERESY
>
> OR NO PHILOSOPHY
>
> WHICH IS SO ABHORRENT
>
> TO THE CHURCH
>
> AS A HUMAN BEING.
>
> From a letter to Lady Gregory

Publishers and printers alike seem to agree among themselves, no matter how divergent their views in other matters, not to publish anything of mine as I wrote it.

> I hear the ruin
> of all space,
> shattered glass
> and toppled masonry,
> and one
> vivid final flame.
>
> *Ulysses*

Secrets, silent, stony, sit in the dark places of our hearts: secrets weary of their tyranny: tyrants waiting to be dethroned.

Ulysses

IT IS A SYMBOL OF IRISH ART. THE CRACKED LOOKING GLASS OF THE SERVANT.

Ulysses

> Welcome. O life! I go to encounter for the millionth time the reality of experience and to forge in the smithy of my soul the uncreated conscience of my race.
>
> *A Portrait of the Artist as a Young Man*

The artist, like the God of the creation, remains within or behind or beyond or above his handiwork, invisible, refined out of existence, indifferent, paring his fingernails.

A Portrait of the Artist as a Young Man

Art is the human disposition of sensible or intelligible matter for an aesthetic end.

A Portrait of the Artist as a Young Man

Once upon a time and it was very good time it was there was a moocow coming down along the road and this moocow that was coming down the road met a nicens little boy named baby tuckoo.

A Portrait of the Artist as a Young Man

Shut your eyes and see.

Ulysses

> Irresponsibility
> is part of
> the pleasure
> of all art:
> it is the part
> the schools
> cannot recognize.
>
> *Ulysses*

> I UNDERSTAND THAT YOU ARE TO TRANSLATE ULYSSES, AND I HAVE COME TO PARIS TO TELL YOU NOT TO ALTER A SINGLE WORD.
>
> To a prospective translator

I have just got a letter asking me why I don't give Bloom a rest. The writer of it wants more Stephen. But Stephen no longer interests me to the same extent. He has a shape that can't be changed.

Frank Budgen
James Joyce and the Making of "Ulysses"

THERE'S ONLY
ONE KIND OF CRITIC
I DO RESENT
THE KIND THAT
AFFECTS TO BELIEVE
THAT I AM WRITING WITH
MY TONGUE IN MY CHEEK.

I DO NOT KNOW WHERE THE BRITISH AND THE AMERICAN PAPERS GET THEIR SCARE HEADLINES ABOUT ME. I HAVE NEVER GIVEN AN INTERVIEW IN MY LIFE AND DO NOT RECEIVE JOURNALISTS. NOR DO I UNDERSTAND WHY THEY SHOULD CONSIDER AN UNREAD WRITER AS GOOD COPY.

No less than twenty-two publishers and printers read the manuscript of Dubliners and when it was at last printed some very kind person bought out the entire edition and had it burnt in Dublin.

> ‘NEVER MIND MY SOUL, JUST MAKE SURE YOU GET MY TIE RIGHT.’

Responding to the painter Patrick Touhy's assertion that he wished to capture Joyce's soul in his portrait of him.

PLENTY TO SEE AND HEAR AND FEEL YET. FEEL LIVE WARM BEINGS NEAR YOU. WARM BEDS: WARM FULL-BLOODED LIFE.

Ulysses

> Whatever else is unsure in this stinking dunghill of a world, a mother's love is not.

A Portrait of the Artist as a Young Man

> Our souls,
> shame-wounded
> by our sins,
> cling to us yet more,
> a woman to her
> love clinging,
> the more the more.
>
> *Ulysses*

'When I makes tea
I makes tea'
as old Mrs Grogan said.
'And when I makes water
I makes water.'

Ulysses

> WHY IS IT THAT WORDS LIKE THESE SEEM DULL AND COLD? IS IT BECAUSE THERE IS NO WORD TENDER ENOUGH TO BE YOUR NAME?
>
> 'The Dead'
> *Dubliners*

> For God's sake
> don't talk politics.
> I'm not interested
> in politics.
> The only thing that
> interests me is style.
>
> Richard Ellman *James Joyce* (1982)

IRELAND SOBER IS IRELAND STIFF.

Finnegans Wake

Full many a flower is born to blush unseen.

Ulysses

The fleshpots of Euston and the hanging garments of Marylebone.

Finnegans Wake

> I AM INCLINED TO THINK THAT BALZAC'S REPUTATION RESTS ON A LOT OF NEAT GENERALIZATIONS ABOUT LIFE.
>
> Frank Budgen
> *James Joyce and the Making of Ulysses*
> (1934)

> 'You behold in me', said Stephen with grim displeasure, 'a horrible example of free thought.'
>
> *Ulysses*

BEWARE

THE HORNS OF A BULL,

THE HEELS OF THE HORSE,

AND THE SMILE OF AN

ENGLISHMAN.

Ulysses

It is as painful to be awakened from a dream as to be born.

Ulysses

> BETTER PASS BOLDLY INTO THAT OTHER WORLD, IN THE FULL GLORY OF PASSION, THAN FADE AND WITHER DISMALLY WITH AGE.
>
> 'The Dead'
> *Dubliners*

'HISTORY', STEPHEN SAID 'IS A NIGHTMARE FROM WHICH I AM TRYING TO AWAKE.'

Ulysses

> WILL SOMEONE TELL ME WHERE I AM LEAST LIKELY TO MEET THESE NECESSARY EVILS?
>
> *Ulysses*

All that falls rises: all that is lost finds its way back; all that forgotten is remembered again.

Finnegans Wake

His eyes were dimmed with tears and, looking humbly up to Heaven, he wept for the innocence he had lost.

A Portrait of the Artist as a Young Man

WE WERE ALL BORN IN THE SAME WAY, BUT WE WILL ALL DIE IN DIFFERENT WAYS.

Ulysses

There is no past, no future; everything flows in an eternal present.

Ulysses

Fall if you will, but rise you must.

Finnegans Wake

I don't want to die. Damn death. Long live life.

Ulysses

Time is, time was, but time will be no more.

A Portrait of the Artist as a Young Man